Commitment Issues in Men

*Understanding His Fear
of Marriage or Fear
of Commitment,
and Helping Him Move
Forward with You
Confidently to Experience
True Intimacy*

by Gabriel Nichols

Table of Contents

Introduction

Although the term "Commitment Phobia" has become nauseatingly common in popular culture, there is a significant number of women who still suffer great anguish because of it. If you are one of these women, trapped in a relationship with a man who balks and scurries like a frightened rabbit when faced with anything remotely concrete or permanent, then I've got two pieces of good news for you: (1) you're not alone... this is quite common, and (2) there are specific things you can do to help him overcome his fear of commitment.

Whether such relationships result because the man hides his problem in the beginning, or the woman is aware of it but thinks she will be the exception that can transform her rogue bad boy into a solid partner, the relationship loses its appeal *fast*, no thanks to the unending emotional rollercoaster. From that point on, every new development has the potential to leave new lifelong scars on the woman, and it becomes significantly harder for her to disengage because of the time and effort she has already invested in the relationship.

However, most women in such relationships aren't just passive observers, but are actively seeking out ways to get through to their men to ensure a happy ending after all the instability and inconsistency. The problem is that every solution that's normally enacted is based on intuition and the women's own idea of what is an appropriate response, often using weak and amateurish pseudo-psychology as a crutch. Sadly, this only brings the relationship closer to the grave, instead of providing any tangible improvement.

In fact, most solutions to such problems are rather **counter-intuitive**, and rely on oodles of patience, mountains of mental strength, and truckloads of willpower. But, hey, if you're sure that your man is really worth the effort, then you've come to the right place. So, are you ready to delve deep into the psyche of your not-so-better-half, and eke out the gem of a man you know he can be? Are you ready to see your vast investment of time and effort in this relationship finally rewarded, and experience the happily-ever-after you've always envisioned for the two of you? Then let's get started!

Chapter 1: Is It *Really* Commitment Phobia?

Now, unfortunately, this term is bandied about so much that women use it to describe just about every aspect of the behavior spectrum of men. Whether the problem is that the guy keeps disappearing and reappearing with more panache than a magician's rabbit or that he refuses to get a cat—a "together decision"—after being so sweet and loving for so many days, the cries of "commitment phobia" can be heard over every rooftop, for miles in any direction you turn.

Therefore, our first order of business becomes understanding this psychological phenomenon better in order to differentiate between commitment phobia and the bitter fact that the guy is just not that into you. A recent study shows that men, on average, prefer to commit themselves to long-term relationships significantly more than women do. It doesn't matter if they're the spitting image of Casanova in thought and deed, most men prefer meaningful commitments and marriage *with the right woman* to perpetual singlehood.

Now, if your man freaks out about making plans together for next Wednesday because he hates planning so far ahead in the future and prefers to live in the moment, he may have commitment issues. If he seems uncomfortable about making plans for you as a pair to attend your cousin's wedding six months down the line, when you're just on your second date—he's normal.

If your guy makes you feel as if his world revolves around your smile and joy, and then suddenly vanishes in a puff of "screw you" smoke, before reappearing with a "I didn't do nothing wrong" grin a week later, complete with a nice tan and a distant whiff of the Caribbean—he has commitment issues. If he tries to back out of a dinner with your family after spending five minutes in the elevator with you— he's normal.

Of course these are humorous exaggerations, except for the Caribbean story which actually happened to a close friend of mine, but the point is that you have to differentiate between the behavior of people who are truly commitment-phobic, and those who simply take longer to open up. Like women, not all guys are the same. I'm sure most of you just rolled your eyes and went "of course they aren't!" So pray tell, why is it that while freaking out, it is very easy to forget this vital piece of information about men?

The best way to figure out true commitment phobia is to set a normal range of behaviors, and then determine where any outlying behavior falls. You also need to talk to other men, and read up on as many similar experiences as you can from valid sources. This is to ensure that you're truly setting a "normal" range, instead of just sets of behavior of what men "should and shouldn't do" according to other people with biases.

For example, if your man does go through every step along the relationship milestones voluntarily and happily, but slower than normal, he may have certain goals in mind (financial, professional, etc.) which he prefers would accompany each succeeding step before marriage—perhaps reaching a certain designation at his firm, or making a certain amount of money—rather than any phobia of commitments. It may seem silly to loving women, but there are plenty of men who feel that way.

The truly commitment-phobic people aren't just anglers or men who are always looking for a chance to use the "bait, hook, and release" tactic, but may be normal people who only regularly freak out at a certain depth into the commitment. For example, not every commitment-phobic guy backs out of getting a pet, or cohabiting with you, but may only freak out in his relationships whenever the "M" word comes up.

Since ordinarily this word comes up only among a limited number of relationships out of the grand total—the pattern may not be so obvious even if you know everything about his past.

On the other hand, if you're in such a relationship, and your plans to get hitched keep getting postponed *ad infinitum*, you may want to entertain the possibility that it's not his emotional maturity that's the problem, as much as *you* yourself. Entertaining yet another line of inquiry, the problem may not be his or your own emotions, but that he simply takes things slower than the average bear, and may require a nudge from you to take the next step.

You must be starting to realize now that the actual world of psychology isn't as cut-and-dry as pseudo-psychological articles and sources from the school of Interweb would have it appear. There are various possible explanations for a single action, and you can often back yourself into a corner through analysis paralysis. Moreover, while actions taken together as patterns do often reveal deeper truths, you need to be sure that every action you include in said pattern actually *belongs* there and is not simply put there by you because it helps make your case. You *do* love your man and wish to end up with him, but the comfortable compulsion to blame the *other* partner for the problems in the relationship is a deeply ingrained one that we all fall prey to at one time or another.

Well, the bad news is this—if you're the problem here, then not much could be changed in this relationship. But here's the good news—if you're not the problem, and your man has commitment issues or even if he's just one of the slower-moving apes in the species, the steps in this guide will help you move in the right direction.

Chapter 2: Understanding Why Men Are So Afraid

Well, it's not just men—there are just as many women who suffer from severe commitment phobia. Moreover, this phobia isn't *nearly* as common among men as pop culture would portray it. In fact, this term was originally coined to denote a tiny segment of the population which had severe mental and psychological problems underlying their relationship experiences. The people who suffered from it often had crippling trust issues and problems bonding with anyone to the point of affecting the quality of their emotional and social life.

If you believe that your man truly has commitment-phobia, and that he isn't just a jerk stringing you along for a place-keeping relationship to keep his bed warm till someone better comes along, you must have noticed some truly panicked behavior and responses on his part. When they must suddenly face the responsibilities of a deepening relationship, some people have genuine panic attacks which trigger fight-or-flight responses. Their behavior may seem inexplicably juvenile, or they may randomly shut you off, or try to take a step forward and end up three steps behind.

Except in cases of the commitment phobic "anglers" and the ones who turn this into pathologically promiscuous sexuality, these behaviors over time almost become an auto-response. It becomes a knee-jerk reaction which occurs before conscious thought. It is then consciously nurtured, out of a belief that it is protecting them from some perceived threat. While the intensity of the phobia varies, it invariably points to deep emotional scarring in the person's past.

There are plenty of reasons why a person gets this way and sometimes the reasons may overlap within a single lifetime. While I'm discussing these reasons, there are others who went through similar troubles but managed to successfully overcome these pains and resume life as mentally healthy individuals.

People with commitment-phobia, on the other hand, either failed to process these pains positively or they emulated maladaptive behavioral patterns which they saw around them. Most importantly, commitment-phobes lacked healthy role models to emulate. So, if one parent was unfaithful and the other was often intoxicated as a result, the growing children could absorb one or both of the behavior patterns and develop a disdain for committed relationships.

It is clear from the example above that the first textbook reason for commitment-phobes is a turbulent family life during their formative years. Since parents or guardians are the first role models of a child, the kind of relationship they have significantly affects our ability to have successful relationships. However, there are many people who outgrow this painful part of their life and go on to forge successful relationships.

A corollary to this is a person who was abused in his childhood, whether physically or mentally. For someone like this, the relationships which should engender feelings of warmth and safety in one's hearts do the opposite. Instead of finding sanctuary through bonds, they feel exposed and vulnerable if they open themselves up too much. Although biological necessity may eventually drive them to have some sort of an intimate relationship with other people at some point, their commitment-phobia nags at them that opening themselves too much to other people will bring back the pain and anguish. Even if they love you, they can't stop thinking that if you show your "true colors" even only once, they're already in too deep and it's time to get out of the relationship.

Another reason why your guy may be commitment-phobic is that he's deathly afraid of failing the responsibilities and expectations a commitment may place on his shoulders. Contrary to what pop culture dictates, studies have shown that men worry about fulfilling their marital duties more often than women. .If your guy thinks that he does a better job being your boyfriend than he could being your husband, and this fear of failing you paralyzes him sufficiently, he could end the relationship at the level where he thinks he performs well, rather than take the next step and fail.

Another reason why men may develop commitment-phobia is their deep sense of independence and the fear of losing the lifestyle they are accustomed to. This reason may be seen in men who grew up under extremely poor conditions and who, through sheer hard work and dedication, later made their mark in the community. They are consequently fiercely independent and self-reliant, attributes which they deeply cherish and are loathe to give up. If they feel that marriage threatens their independence they become commitment-phobic.

Another corollary to this is the much shallower reason of not wanting to lose their lifestyle. These men adequately recognize that married men do not have the same lifestyle as single men or even boyfriends have. I'm not talking about sleeping around here, though that may be a factor. Such men are satisfied with their lives as they are, and don't wish for any change in the equation—and so are afraid of taking their commitment to the next level.

Another popular reason among commitment-phobes (who had normal childhoods) is that they have been hurt by a relationship before. Maybe they were deeply committed before, but were either cheated on or their partners simply walked out. In the normal span of a life, given enough relationships, people experience both these events at least once. While most people process these things somewhat successfully, some people get twisted after going through such an experience. In such people, they give rise to fears of rejection and/or severe trust issues, all of which lead to commitment-phobia.

One of the last sub-sections which we will discuss is those of the men who aren't commitment-phobic because something happened that damaged them, but are sociopathically unable to formulate or treasure the importance of bonds with other people. While some among them sufficiently gain a rational understanding of the importance of relationships, others show little regard for bonds beyond self-satisfaction and gain. However, calling this subset *commitment-phobic* would be erroneous, since they aren't afraid of making a commitment as much as being psychologically or even neurologically unable to understand their importance in human social or personal life. The root causes behind this state, and whether it is purely psychological or does in fact have neurological causes, are still being studied in greater detail—but attempting to have a long lasting bond with this set is beyond your capabilities.

Chapter 3: Identifying the Underlying Root Cause

One of the biggest troubles with commitment-phobic people is that they tend to compartmentalize their lives quite successfully. So, while you may have met some of his more recent friends, you haven't met any of his family or childhood buddies who are still close with him. Or, while you may have met people close to him on the professional side of his life, you haven't met any who form a part of his personal life. Again, pay attention here—if this isn't the case and you've met everyone, chances are that he isn't commitment-phobic. Or else while you may meet everyone, none of them *really* talked to you about his past in any detail since he severely dislikes that.

Anyway, with all this compartmentalization, it becomes rather difficult to chalk out the source of his commitment-phobia. Since parents and friends are an important source of information, limitations upon these resources severely hinders your ability to figure out the root of the problem and get to repairing it.

Therefore, the biggest available resource to you is your guy himself. Though you've been paying close attention, you need to step it up further without letting him sense the change. If he feels scrutinized, he'll be out of the door before you can scream "Hakuna Matata."

Whenever the two of you spend time together, pay attention to his reactions to different subjects. Are there movies with common themes to which he reacts more strongly, or overly sarcastically, than usual? Are there news articles or TV shows where he holds harsher or stronger opinions than he usually displays? Do certain types of families or couples draw more ire or annoyance from him, or stronger emotions, than usual? If your man behaves perfectly in almost every aspect, do specific events trigger outright signs of phobia in him? Does he hate waiting? If he shares about events in his past, does he control his emotions while he's talking about them?

These observations, would help you narrow down the source of his phobia, because no two experiences and commitment-phobes are alike. If he deliberately arranges situations so that he would be the centre of attention, it could point to fears of rejection or of being left unacknowledged. If so, his commitment-phobia may arise from the fear of losing his individuality within a marriage or similar bonds. If he's excessively, and often needlessly, rebellious then his phobia could stem from overbearing parents or lack of any tangible freedoms as a child, and so he's afraid of being imprisoned by another relationship after he's freed himself from his parents.

In the absence of other sources, this is how you'll piece together parts of his psyche and the triggers associated with his particular brand of commitment phobia. If he doesn't want children, or freaks out if you talk about getting a pet together, his phobia may arise from the thought of his own familial preferences being squashed in favor of his partner's in a marriage. On the other hand, if he seems to back away further as you get deeper into a relationship, he may feel his phobia surfacing from a sense of being smothered by your expectations and sense of responsibilities which you may be consciously or unconsciously placing on him.

Apart from plain observations, if he decides to share the experiences of tumultuous days at work or other spheres of his life, you could try asking analytical questions in order to better understand his mindset. This is helpful because people with the strongest commitment issues don't deal with this problem in one aspect of their lives but it tends to loosely splash over into other aspects as well. How does he react to opportunities around him? If he seems to be angling for employment opportunities elsewhere, he may be looking for an excuse out of your relationship, unless he's explicitly spoken to you about moving with him when that change happens.

As I've mentioned before, the largest challenge for you will be to identify and separate the actions motivated by his phobia from others that form part of his personality. While you keep an eye on him, don't be too ready to attribute an action to commitment-phobia unless it makes logical sense within the pattern.

In the search for the source of his phobia, you will have to question or probe him discreetly through your intuition, but the information you glean will have to be analyzed through cold, hard logic. That will only be possible if you remove your own ego out of the equation, and emotionally distance yourself from the process but not from him.

Chapter 4: Helping Him Deal with His Phobia

The biggest problem with helping other people deal with psychological issues is that we tend to do so while placing ourselves at the center of their universe. With commitment-phobic people who can't be oriented or manipulated, it has to happen on its own. Plus, it's a slightly sickening feeling to accept the idea that an ex-partner did so much damage that it led to psychological issues in your guy. The instinct to start comparing may lead to an emotional outburst and this may drive him away at Mach speed, instead of helping him get over it.

Try to understand at this point that it isn't the person who does the damage but the experience itself. Rape victims often find it extremely difficult to get over that violent event, and develop severe intimacy and boundary issues so strong that many of them can't even stand the touch of their own spouses or other trusted partners. It's a reaction which has nothing to do with the people involved. Children who come from broken homes or toxic childhood atmospheres spent the innocent parts of their early life investing in relationships which *did* return some warmth and good memories, before blowing up in smoke. *That's* what some commitment-phobes are afraid of. Whether consciously or subconsciously, they fear the isolation and desolation which accompanies the implosion of a bond upon which they have learned to depend and rely on.

Another problem with helping men get over commitment issues is that many women believe that nurturing and loving relationships will somehow heal them. While that may be true in a very loose sense, or in later stages of their recuperation, it's balderdash for the earlier stages. The problem isn't that they can't appreciate warmth, but that they believe it won't last and so they would rather not depend on it.

The following steps which I'll discuss won't just address one of the many sources, but rather attempt to cover as many of them as possible, in the event that you were either unable to, or misinterpreted, the root of their phobia.

Now the one thing I *won't* do (though you should still do this for your own sake) is tell you to get in the best shape of your life. People who truly suffer from commitment-phobia aren't concerned about the shape you're in—if that were the problem then they wouldn't be with you in the first place. In the off chance that your man isn't committing to you because you aren't in the most drop-dead gorgeous shape of your life, is that the sort of person you really want to swear yourself to for the rest of your life? Wouldn't you rather have someone beside you who values both your external *and* internal traits?

However, the first step is getting your own life. If you're too deeply involved in your relationship, while your partner has a life outside of you as well, he is probably overwhelmed by the thought of him being your sole social contact with the outside world. Believe it or not, that's an immense responsibility just barely handled properly even by healthy men, and far beyond the capability of one who is struggling just to remain in a commitment. So, make sure that you stay connected with your own friends as well, and expand his social life by introducing him to your close social network too. This helps ease his mind about where he fits in your existence, and gives him more stable points of contact with your life.

The previous step fits neatly into the next one—show him off, but don't cling on too tightly. Make sure you let him know at every point just how proud you are to have him in your life, and that you appreciate his presence and everything he brings to the table as well as how safe he makes you feel. At the same time, whether you're at social gatherings or even just spending time by yourselves at home, be sure to give him plenty of space if he's doing something or talking to someone. Don't play the part of the jealous or clingy girlfriend, and don't bombard him with questions at every turn. Again, in this instance, I'm assuming that you've differentiated between commitment-phobia and the inability to keep it in his pants. If his problem's the latter, nothing can help you there.

When you're alone with him, provide him with a safe atmosphere. If you cook, try and figure out his comfort foods and attempt to replicate them for him. If you disagree with him, even if you do so strongly, find loving and constructive ways to get the message across rather than just throw criticisms at his face. Remember that the tone of the message matters just as much as the content—so maintain a caring and calm attitude during any disagreement. If you're ever having a fight, and he seems to be losing his composure, back off for a little bit and let him regain his footing before continuing with the conversation. Heated emotions lead to impulsive decisions—and the one thing you want to avoid at all costs is to let his commitment phobic instincts kick in at this juncture.

Whenever you're talking to him about anything, give him your undivided attention rather than distributing it between your work, your phone, the TV, and everything else. Let him *feel* that his voice and opinions are valued and treasured, and that you're always interested in what he has to say.

If you're sure that his problem is commitment phobia, and that he's not just a compulsive cheater—never give him the opportunity to doubt your loyalty to him. This may require some skilled maneuvering back and forth if he displays unnecessary jealousy from time to time regarding your social companions, but that's a price you need to pay if you wish to achieve your goals with him.

Whether his problems stem from his childhood or his past partners, you need to distinguish yourself from the herd and prove to him—yes, *prove* to him—that you will never hurt him or betray his trust. This will require significant investments of time and effort, because he will have placed his trust in other people he thought were safe before as well. However, when he starts seeking you out in times of turbulence, you know you've made significant strides in this direction.

If his problems stem from fears of losing his independence, giving him sufficient space to be himself and thus disproving fears that the two of you would have to disappear into a single anthropomorphic blob after getting married should be sufficient. However, if his problem is that he fears

31

for the life he built on his own, nothing short of you proving yourself to be completely self-reliant and independent as well will assuage those fears. On the other hand, if his phobia stems from his losing his current lifestyle, well either the space you provide will help him get over them or the time spent with you will prove to him that any changes that will happen will be an improvement. Short of that, I'm sorry to say, nothing apart from him actually mentally maturing will solve that fear. And that's not something you can push or direct, but it has to be a change which he's willing to undergo and for which he's receptive.

If his problems originate from his fears of failure as a husband, you need to lower your expectations and show greater appreciation for the steps which he does take to keep you happy, even if they are small— particularly if these are skills which would translate through to marriage. If he makes you feel safe and warm, make sure that he knows that loud and clear. Compliment any skills which you believe would make him a good husband, without using those words. In fact, till the situation changes drastically, don't mention marriage or anything related to it in any way at all. Even avoid making concrete plans too far into the future. If you have a wedding to attend in the next six months, don't push him to make any plans as your "plus one". Just mention the idea to him if you feel you've been together long enough, and tell him that he has plenty of time to decide if he would be interested. If he isn't, don't make a meal of it, just tell him that you'll miss him and go with another friend. Best case scenario: It incites a bit of jealousy in your man, and he changes his mind about the event.

Chapter 5:   Sealing the Deal and Getting What You Want

If you want him to get over his commitment-phobia and propose to you, the first thing you need to do is toss out any strong expectations you may have about married life and how it's going to be for you. There may come a point in the future where you may get exactly what you wish, but for now you need to figure out his image rather than assert your own.

If that seems slightly off-putting, then you may not be as ready to go through this process as you originally thought yourself to be. However, if you understand why this is necessary—you're truly mentally prepared to go the distance for this guy. And I sincerely hope he's worth the trouble.

The first step in all of these matters is to subtly find out if your guy has had any image in his mind about married life, and if he has any expectations related to it. The best time for this sort of conversation isn't in public, but at a casual and private *tête-à-tête* between the two of you—preferably when he is slightly intoxicated so that his mental guard is lowered. Make sure that any questions regarding such matters don't have any strings or expectations of the future attached from your end. Chances may be that he may never have thought about such matters in detail, and so you may have to break the conversation down from your end into smaller bits and pieces. For example, instead of asking him what his ideal bride would be like, play silly games like kiss-screw-marry with him. Give him options of celebrities which you are both well aware of, and remember his answers for marry. Each time you get an answer, be sure to ask him why he would choose a particular man or women for each activity, and do the same whenever your turn comes around. However, in your turns, either pick choices who are physically similar to him or those who have character traits in common with your guy.

In this fashion, you can figure out his preferences without pushing any expectations to get married any time soon. Now, right from the start, I want you to be clear about one thing—this may be a long term project, and you need to be prepared for the invariable periods of hopelessness. However, if you can perform each step of this guide to your utmost capability, your patience will indubitably be rewarded one way or another.

Once you've figured out his preferences, try to orient your own personality closer to his ideal. Don't make this change in a day, but space it out over a matter of months. If he mentioned any overt changes, like a preference for blonde hair over your brunette locks, don't switch over the next day. Instead wait for a month or longer to put any physical changes in place. Chances are that his memory of the conversation will be dimmed by then, and he won't connect the dots and figure out what you're up to.

After having shifted your own personality and looks slightly closer to his ideal, check and see if he starts warming up to you even more, or if he looks at you any differently than before. The point here isn't that you've hidden who you are to please him—but that you've gotten the physical differences out of the way so that he can better appreciate your qualities as a partner. Again, if your physical appearance displeased him so much, he wouldn't have been with you in the first place.

If he starts responding more to you, and feels safer around you thanks to the steps from the last chapter, he should start treating you as more indispensable than he did before. Do not let this get to your head and change your behavior at this point. That's precisely what happened to him before, and he will run like the wind if he senses the same pattern re-emerging. Hold the fort, and deepen the same behavior which made him feel more secure around you. At this point, nurturing him further and proffering more affection may yield positive results and get him to open up even more. However, don't be clingy, and don't play the jealous girl.

Once you're more indispensable, take him further a step at a time. If the two of you aren't living together, try spending more time at his place or get him to spend more time at yours. Make sure that he has comfortable space for his stuff at your place, so that he isn't tempted to bolt away every so often to pick stuff up from his residence. At the same time, don't leave too much stuff at his place, and for everything that you do leave—take his permission before hand. If he denies permission, don't pout or sulk but take it in your stride. Smile, thank him for considering it, and move on from that conversation as if nothing of import took place.

Slowly, but surely, show him the advantages of living under the same roof in a loving and committed relationship—whether it's cohabitation, or marriage. Make his life with you more comfortable and rewarding than his outside life seems to be. Once you can get the two of you living together, in all but name, get a pet for the two of you. Not only will it provide an additional source of affection for him, prompting him to open up further, but it will also provide another connection tying you indispensably to his life. If neither of you wish to have pets, then try and officially move in together in a house with both of your names on the lease. The point here is to create a life which is as close to being married, without the tag of being married.

After this life is settled and consistently working out for the two of you for a few months, you need to spend more relaxed time with him, have a few drinks, and figure out if his intentions have budged in the slightest. Don't push him or ask him if he's ready for marriage—instead, play coy, be cute, and ask him questions like "So, would your ideal wife be anything like me?" and so on. By this point, if everything's gone well, he should be able to at least joke around about the idea with you in a comfortable setting. Through all of this, you also need to make sure that your family and friends put no pressure on him to take the leap, and any push which may come from their end needs to be absorbed by you instead.

Once you've created a life which is indispensable for him, one which is as close to being married without actually being so as possible, you will have reached a point where you need to move on to the next step. This will entail continuing along the same path as before, while starting to joke around about getting married without any hints of being serious about it.

If you choose to get started on this path—start joking with him about stuff related to married life. So, for example, you could toy with him about stuff you would do to him in bed in your white dress on your first night as a married couple, or you could jokingly call yourself Mrs. *Insert His Family Name*, and so on. At other times, you could sigh and exclaim that you have everything you could possibly want, except for being able to call yourself his. Don't ever turn the sentence and complain about not being able to call him yours, and don't use the word "forever" regardless. No matter what, avoid the trigger words and find a way to get your message across without sulking or moaning or putting him through emotional drama. Nor should you use any negative methods too often. Remember that you will not be able to bully, threaten, cajole, or harass him into getting married. He needs to realize that he's already married in all but name, that he actually likes it, that he treasures you and wants to give you everything possible in life that he can, and then ask you to get married of his own volition.

Another thing which you can start doing is to compliment him on skills and attributes which would make him a great husband or dad. If the two of you have a pet, and he got angry because someone mistreated the pet—kiss him, and tell him he would make an amazing father, etc. If he gets jealous because someone flirted with you or stared at you,

40

start singing "Single Ladies" by Beyonce to tease him. In essence, keep reinforcing the idea that things will get better from that point on, if only he takes the next step, and that he's more than capable of handling that change.

While these steps should push him to take the next step by themselves, you can also attempt to reinforce a sense of urgency in him. If you're ever lost in thought about this and feeling sad, don't always change your expression immediately as he walks in. Let him catch you seeming melancholic sometimes, before changing your expression and smiling for him. After a while, if he asks you if everything's okay, simply tell him that you were just thinking about when you were a kid and you used to dream about being married to your perfect man by this point. Then, just kiss him and tell him something along the lines of "at least I'm already with my dream man, even if I'm not married." Whatever you choose to communicate with him, do so in a positive and relaxed manner so that he doesn't feel like he's being strung along.

If your guy still doesn't respond to the sense of urgency after a few months, and you're starting to get impatient, you have one last step left to take which could deliver faster results—propose to him instead. Unless you wish to wait further, and let things take their own course no matter how long that may take, the only option left after all this preparation will be to take matters in your own hands. While this may not be the way you imagined it to be, make sure that you give him plenty of time to think about it after the proposal. Also make sure to tell him that if he declines, you'll understand his point of view and that you won't begrudge him for it, but that if he decides to accept, he will be there as faithfully and unerringly for you as you will be for him.

Conclusion

Though this book attempts to provide as much knowledge about this process as possible, the one thing it cannot convey is the depth of commitment this entire journey will require of you. Although I can readily understand that you would not take these steps unless you were entirely sure, I hope you can understand that you will be investing a significant portion of your immediate future into a relationship which may end in the two of you parting ways despite your best efforts.

Beyond that, I also hope that you aren't among the women who have hitched their ride to a womanizer in the hopes of reforming him—that will never happen if he was and still is a womanizer right after meeting you. If you were the woman he was going to marry, you wouldn't need this or any other guide to make that happen. Indeed, you would be the one trying to hit the brakes because he'd be the one moving at breakneck speed.

In the end, before you try to embark on a journey without an end, I would strongly urge taking some time on your own and figuring out exactly what makes this man worth the effort for you. Often, women who are in relationships with commitment-phobic men tend to have a pattern originating from their own deep-seated psychological issues. Since commitment-phobes take time to open up or entertain the possibility of a long-term relationship which would surround them with responsibilities, their finest qualities are often not visible to their partners. That begs the question—what exactly did you see in your man for it to be worth going through all this anguish?

However, if you have an answer ready and waiting at the tip of your tongue, let me say this—whether you go fast or slow isn't what freaks out such men. The scariest part, for such people are *labels* and *tags*, rather than actual responsibilities. They would rather be life-long boyfriends with all the functions of a husband, than be called a husband prematurely. Moreover, since the modern age looks more kindly on cohabitation than society did in earlier times, the sense of urgency to make a lasting commitment has further reduced their need to get over their fear of the labels. So, instead, you need to trick their own mind into thinking of *you* with the label, instead of trying to tag them with it. Once they start thinking of you as their wife or husband, you've already won the race.

Finally, I'd like to thank you for purchasing this book! If you found it helpful, I'd greatly appreciate it if you'd take a moment to leave a review on Amazon. Thank you!

Printed in Great Britain
by Amazon

15946633R00031